ONE GREEN BOTTLE

Andersen Young Readers' Library

HAZEL TOWNSON

ONE GREEN BOTTLE

Illustrated by David McKee

Andersen Press · London

First published in 1987 by
Andersen Press Limited,
62-65 Chandos Place, London WC2

British Library Cataloguing in Publication Data
Townson, Hazel
One green bottle.
I. Title II. McKee, David
832'.914[J] PZ7

ISBN 0 86264-164-0

Printed and bound in Great Britain
by Anchor Brendon Limited, Tiptree, Essex

Contents

For the Bury Metro Children's Libraries Team

ALISON DAVIES
MAVIS DENNY
JEAN HAMER
ISABEL HANNAH
KATHLEEN PACEY
ANDREW STACHNIEWSKI

and remembering with great affection CELIA COOK.

I

All in the Game

'Why isn't he in the school football team?' Tim Evans's Aunt Maisie asked.

'Why *aren't* you in the school football team?' Tim's mother asked Tim.

'Because I'm not good enough,' said Tim.

'Not good enough?' cried Aunt Maisie indignantly. 'When your Uncle Cyril was Cleckhampton Rovers' goalie for seven years?'

'Of course he's good enough,' retorted Mrs Evans, who was Uncle Cyril's sister. 'He's just lazy, that's all. Won't be bothered to practise.'

'Yes, I will!' protested Tim. 'I mean, I would if I was good enough.'

'Well, you never will be good enough if you don't practise,' said his mother, and there was no answer to that.

Tim Evans had lost another argument. Worse, he had been made to feel inadequate; even more inadequate than he had been made to feel yesterday when he dropped the milk jug, left his scarf on the bus and trod on next door's kitten's tail. Sighing, Tim retired to his room and got on with his secret hobby, which was inventing games.

At the present moment Tim was working on a game called REDUNDO. Two or more players shook dice and moved round a board with the object of being first to get a job. There were various aids and obstacles on the way, such as: 'New soap factory opens—move forward three squares' or 'More local government cuts—go back to DOLE'. The snag was, it was difficult to add refinements to the game without actually playing it properly, and so far Tim was the only player. He badly needed advice and encouragement. Tim had hoped to recruit his friend Doggo Barker, but Tim's mother would not let Doggo penetrate any further than the kitchen, so that was that. Tim had no intention of fetching his game into the kitchen. He had vowed that his family must never set eyes on the REDUNDO board until he had sold it to a top toy manufacturer for at least a four-figure sum. That would show them! That would prove who was adequate and who wasn't! Tim's dad might well have a hush-hush job at the Helmuth Research Establishment (as Tim's mother was fond of reminding the neighbours) but that did not mean to say Lewis Evans was a genius. He was probably just the test-tube washer-up for some top scientist, or the bloke who mixed the guard-dogs' dinners. No wonder he would never talk about his work.

'Tim!' Mrs Evans yelled up the stairs. 'Your Uncle Cyril's here! Come and say hello to your Uncle Cyril.'

Tim trudged reluctantly downstairs. This interruption had cost him another great idea. He had just been about to write: 'Miners' strike—miss seven throws'. Or should it be: 'Teachers' go-slow—move forward two'? He couldn't quite decide which. At this rate his parents weren't going to live to see his triumph.

'Now then, Tim!' boomed Uncle Cyril, slapping the poor lad heartily on the shoulder.

'Hi, Uncle Cyril!' mumbled Tim, wincing with pain.

'I'm not all *that* high; only six foot one!' Uncle Cyril guffawed. Tim should have known better than to give him the opportunity for one of his terrible jokes.

'Well now,' Uncle Cyril went on, ignoring the stony silence, 'I've just been reading an ad. in the paper for your school's Music Festival. I don't mind coming to hear you sing in the choir, so you can sell me a couple of tickets if you like.'

'I'm not *in* the choir,' said Tim.

'Not in the choir?' cried Uncle Cyril, aghast. 'And you with a name like Evans? Let me tell you, your dad sang in the *Messiah* every Christmas until you were born.' Turning to Tim's mother, he asked: 'Why isn't he in the choir?'

Mrs Evans scowled at Tim. 'Well, why aren't you in

the choir?'

'Because I can't sing,' said Tim.

'CAN'T SING? Three generations of Welsh blood on his dad's side, and he can't sing?' Uncle Cyril looked ready to collapse.

'Of course he can sing!' snapped Mrs Evans. 'He's just lazy, that's all. Can't be bothered to go to the rehearsals. He'd rather shut himself up in his bedroom with a bundle of daft comics.'

'I'm going out,' said Tim. 'I'm going round to Doggo's.'

'And I don't know why you can't call that boy by his proper name. Eustace, isn't it? Your tea will be ready in half an hour, so don't you dare be late.'

Tim slammed the door as hard as he could, and was rewarded with a shaft of dazzling inspiration. 'World War Three breaks out—move forward twenty spaces.' Or better still: 'World War Three breaks out—drop dead!'

2

The Wrong Shop

On his way to Doggo's, Tim had to pass the 'FAIR GAME' shop window. The centre-piece of the window display was a set of tall ivory chessmen coloured red and white. Behind that was suspended a larger-than-life Monopoly board with a brimming bucket of Monopoly money underneath it, and crossed billiard-cues at either side. Around the rest of the window lay various other games in brightly-coloured boxes; packs of cards; table-tennis outfits; shuttlecocks; yoyos; roulette wheels and giant dice.

Tim could not help stopping to stare, and soon all sorts of exciting possibilities were bouncing about his brain, sparking off a bright hallucination. The chessmen were gone, and there instead lay his REDUNDO board with intricate carvings of the characterful unemployed plodding their way to salvation across brilliantly-coloured squares.

Tim sighed deeply through a wistful smile. Then the chessmen swam back into focus—and on an impulse, Tim hurried into the shop.

Sam Snyder, the proprietor, was gift-wrapping a

Ludo game for a kind old lady who must be someone's great-granny. He frowned at Tim over the string-dispenser, forcefully conveying the impression that he knew exactly what Tim would be up to, given half a chance, but he needn't think he would get away with it. Tim fidgeted among the books—(*Pukka Poker*; *Mah-Jongg for the Million; Pontoon, Bridge and Other Diversions*)—whilst great-granny scrabbled in her handbag for cheque-book and pen. By the time she had altered the date on the cheque, turned out all her pockets for the bank-card and verified the price another twice, Tim had lost his courage and was slinking towards the door. But that made Sam Snyder suspicious. By now, the lad probably had a ping-pong ball up each sleeve and a pocketful of best quality Fetherflite darts.

'Hey, you! Come here!'

Tim swung round to face the counter, blushing as guiltily as if he had planned to mug great-granny on her way out.

'What do you want then, eh?' Sam Snyder was busy frisking Tim with his eyes whilst the old lady tottered happily on her way.

Tim took a deep breath, which steadied his nerve and gave him time to think. At last he managed to blurt out:

'I've invented a game!'

'Oh you have, have you?' Sam Snyder's sarcasm

could have felled a sturdy oak. 'Well, go and play it, then.'

The doorbell was already pinging with the next bona fide customer, which Tim patently was not.

But now, having gathered his courage, Tim did not intend to leave without some sort of satisfaction. He drew from his pocket a dog-eared, grubby sheet of much-folded paper, which he laid reverently on the counter.

'It's called REDUNDO. These are the rules and stuff. I know you're busy, Mr Snyder, but I'll call back later today when you've had time to read it, and I'll bring the board. I'll have managed to finish it by then.'

So saying, Tim fled, colliding with the incoming customer who lurched into a Magnetic Fishing set, sending shoals of little metal fish in a frantic surge to freedom.

Sam Snyder's eyes turned upwards to the giant frisbee hanging from the ceiling. 'Kids!' he exclaimed, screwing up the precious sheet of REDUNDO rules and hurling it into his waste-bin.

3

First Tastes of Human Error

''Uman error, that's what ruins everything,' declared Mrs Figgins from next door. 'You've only to look at aeroplanes. They can fill 'em up with all this clever stuff like radars and black boxes and I-don't-know-what, but if the pilot drops his glasses, or chokes on a fish-bone, you've had it! What I say is, you can't get away from 'uman error wherever you go.'

Tim's mother shivered. She had been telling Mrs Figgins that they were thinking of going to Spain for a holiday next summer, but now she was not so sure. The Evans family were new to the mysteries of flying, and maybe things had better stay that way.

'Yes, well—I'm just going round to the supermarket,' decided Mrs Evans in an attempt to get rid of her caller.

Mrs Figgins snorted loudly. 'Huh! Now there's 'uman error if ever I saw it! All them fancy machines for adding up your bill and taking away your change, and what happens? Daft girl hits the wrong keys and you get diddled. 'Uman error, that's what!' Her eyes narrowed as she added darkly, 'Let's hope there's none of it up at Hellmouth, that's all I can say!'

'Hellmouth' was the local nickname for the Helmuth Research Establishment where Tim's dad worked, and where it was suspected, but by no means confirmed, that lethal germs were being manufactured which could wipe out the whole of Russia some windy weekend.

Suddenly Mrs Figgins spotted Tim, who was hunched in an armchair reading his *Dandy*.

'Why can't he go to the supermarket for you?'

'Oh, you know what boys are. He's too lazy, that's why.'

'You never asked me!' protested Tim indignantly. 'I'll go if you like.'

'No thanks! We don't want to be sending search parties out. We want our dinner today, not next week. Anyway, if we're talking about human error. . . . '

Tim did not wait to hear any more. He threw his comic down disgustedly and marched off to collect his anorak. He would nip round to the 'FAIR GAME' shop and see if Mr Snyder had had time to look at REDUNDO yet. After all, he had had the board for a whole day now.

Mr Snyder was alone in the shop, re-packing a set of top quality, genuine wooden draughts which a customer had examined and rejected. He was cross to start with, and his mood did not improve when Tim asked

eagerly, 'Did you have time to look at it, then?'

'Look at what?'

'My game—REDUNDO.'

'Oh, that! What do *you* think, son?'

'You mean, you haven't even . . . ?'

'Look, laddie, I'm supposed to be running a business here, not a Citizens' Advice Bureau. That doorbell never stops pinging from morning to night.'

'It's not pinging now,' Tim pointed out reasonably enough.

Mr Snyder flushed a dull red. 'Cheeky young scamp! Go on, clear out of it!'

'I want my game back first.'

'Well, it'll be where you left it.'

Tim looked down the side of the counter, where he remembered having propped his board, but it was not there.

'It's gone!'

'Well, somebody's pinched it, then. I certainly haven't moved it.'

Tim's bitter disappointment was succeeded by alarm. 'They can't have pinched it! You don't understand—it's very important, is that board. I've got to have it back.'

'Shouldn't have left it there, then, should you? *I* didn't ask you to. I can't be responsible for stuff left lying in the shop. I lose enough of my own stock to shoplifters, and that's a fact.'

'Shoplifters?' Tim's voice had taken on a note of horror. 'You mean, a shoplifter's taken my board? Well, have you any idea who it could have been, Mr Snyder? Which customers were in the shop yesterday?'

'Now, that's a daft question, isn't it, son? Be reasonable! Do you think Father Christmas can remember what he's put down every chimney? 'Course he can't! He's got too much on his mind, like me.'

Tim clutched at this thread of hope. 'In that case—

suppose you had so much on your mind that you moved my board without thinking? You could have tidied it away with some other boards. Sort of—a case of human error.'

Sam Snyder found that idea downright insulting. 'I'll give you a taste of human error, you young monkey!' He started forward with goodness knows what fell purpose in mind, but just then a delivery man staggered in with two dozen sets of 'Scrabble' and a box of spinning-tops, and Tim was lost sight of in the rush.

4

Dark Suspicions

Doggo Barker was on the playing field, swinging from a piece of his mother's clothes-line which he had attached to a tree.

'Hey, Doggo!' Tim had to shout three times to attract his friend's attention. 'Want to come and help me catch a shoplifter?' It was a desperately anxious invitation.

'Too easy!' boasted Doggo. 'There's more shoplifters in the world than proper customers.' All the same, Doggo jumped down from his rope, which managed to swing wide and slap backwards on to Tim, catching him right across the neck.

'Ooops! Sorry!'

'Hey, that hurt!' A great red weal immediately began to rise on Tim's neck, which he fingered tenderly as he told the tale of the missing REDUNDO board.

Doggo was not impressed. 'Can't you make another? Surely you've not forgotten already what you put on it? We've plenty of cardboard at our house, and you can borrow our Eileen's felt-tips.'

'It wasn't cardboard; it was a good piece of formica I found under some rubbish at the back of our shed, and I stuck proper drawing paper over it. Anyway, that's not the point. If I don't get that board back, somebody else could pinch my idea. It's worth a fortune.'

'Gerraway!' grinned Doggo.

'It's true! You know the bloke who invented "Monopoly"? He's a multi-millionaire now.'

'Sure he is!' Doggo's grin widened.

'Honestly, he's shovelling money in. And my game's as good as that, if not better. Anybody who know anything about games will tell you.'

'Sam Snyder doesn't seem to have been very taken with it.'

'He never even looked at it.'

Doggo's eyes suddenly brightened. 'How do you know he didn't?'

'He said so, didn't he?'

'Yeah, and he once told me he'd sold out of fireworks when I knew bloomin' well he hadn't. Just because our Eileen put a banger through his letter-box.'

'You mean . . . ?'

'I mean, suppose Sam Snyder's the one who's pinched your game? He'd know just what to do with it, an' all. He'd know how to set about getting a patent, or whatever you call it, so that nobody can copy it. He'd know how to have all the boards and pieces properly

made and dished out round all the games shops. He'd even know how to advertise it. For a bloke in his position, all that sort of stuff would be as easy as falling off one of his own warpy old skateboards. You could be buying a REDUNDO set yourself in a few weeks' time, and Snyder would be raking in the profits.'

'Never!' yelled Tim, adding, with less conviction, 'Do you reckon?'

'Believe me, it's the only answer. Nobody else but Snyder would think of such a thing, and anyway, nobody else could ever have sneaked out of that shop with a great board under their arm and not be spotted by beady-eyed Sam.'

Tim looked stunned. There was a long, agonising pause before he said:

'Well, that's fraud and stealing and a lot besides, and he needn't think he's going to get away with it. I'll show him!'

'That's the spirit!' grinned Doggo, relishing the prospect of battle. 'Now you're talking!'

'I'll murder him!' growled Tim, already rushing off in the direction of 'FAIR GAME'. But Doggo dragged him to a halt. 'Hang about! You can't just go barging in there, chucking accusations around. He'll only deny them. You want a proper plan. In fact, what you want to do is frighten him into a confession. It's the only way.'

Wild as he was, Tim could not help feeling this idea was even wilder. Nothing would frighten Sam Snyder, except possibly the Income Tax man. But Doggo went on thoughtfully, 'You could do it, an' all! If I had a "highly secret" dad like you have, I'd frighten Snyder all right.'

'What do you mean, a "highly secret" dad? He's not a bloomin' spy.'

'He works at Hellmouth, doesn't he? Who know what goes on behind them armed patrols and electrified fences and remote-controlled gates? If you played your cards right, you could reduce old Snyder to a trembling blob of jelly.'

'Oh, yeah!' sneered Tim. 'I could borrow my dad's Death Ray out of the bathroom cabinet.'

'Hey—that remark's not as daft as you think! It's just given me an idea.'

Tim groaned, and was about to protest that he would have nothing to do with Doggo's idea, when suddenly Mrs Evans and Aunt Maisie hove into view.

'Told you where he'd be, didn't I?' Aunt Maisie cried.

'Here, our Tim!' shouted Mrs Evans angrily. 'Have you gone off with that piece of formica that your dad was going to fix on top of my washer? Because if you have, you can jolly well fetch it back, double-quick.'

Before Tim could reply, Aunt Maisie shrieked:

'Oooh, what's he done to his neck?'

'What *have* you done to your neck?' Tim's mother asked Tim.

'I tried to hang myself,' mumbled Tim, 'but it didn't work, worse luck!'

5

Instant Death

'Whatever's this, then?' Tim asked, as Doggo emerged from his house clutching a bottle of dark green liquid.

'Shampoo.'

'Well, we're not going to scare anybody with that.'

'Don't you be too sure!' Doggo turned the bottle round so that Tim could read the label. At the top was a garish picture of a multi-coloured skull-and-cross-bones over the bright red letters: 'GLOLOX'. Under that, in two lines of thick black type, were the words:

INSTANT DEATH
TO DANDRUFF!

Doggo's dad ran the local barber's shop and often brought home free samples of shampoos and various other hair preparations that travellers had tried to persuade him to use. This one was the very latest, not yet on the market.

'If we cut the bottom line off that label,' Doggo explained, 'Sam Snyder won't know this stuff from Nitro-Glycerine or Plague-Infested Gooseberry Wine.

We'll just drop the merest hint that you may have pinched it from your dad, who works at Hell-mouth . . . .'

'But my dad wouldn't bring anything home from there. They get searched all the time. They even check on his sandwich box.'

'So what? Sam Snyder's not to know that, is he? He'll think your dad sneaked the INSTANT DEATH out to sell to the IRA or something. It's my bet Snyder will give us the benefit of the doubt *and* your REDUNDO board when he sees that bottle.'

'You're mad!' exploded Tim. 'You can't go around threatening folks like that.'

'Who's threatening folks? It's only shampoo.'

'Well, you'd never get away with it. And anyway, you'd land my dad in a right load of trouble.'

'It's nothing to do with your dad. My dad's more likely to be in trouble than yours if anything goes wrong. But nothing's going to go wrong.'

'That's all *you* know! Suppose you do happen to scare Snyder, and he hands my board back? What's he going to do then? As soon as we've left the shop he's going to ring up the police and tell them there's a deadly bottle at large from Hellmouth and my dad's pinched it.'

'He won't do that. Because as soon as we've got your board back we'll explain it was just a joke. Sam Snyder runs a games shop. He's in the entertainments business, isn't he? So he should be able to see the funny side.'

'*You* should be in the entertainment business,' grumbled Tim. 'You could earn a living making up tall stories for fifth-rate comics.'

'You're not *scared* of Snyder, by any chance, are you?' grinned Doggo.

'Me? Scared?'

They argued on for a while, Tim suggesting (and Doggo demolishing) more and more possible snags, until in the end Tim began to think his REDUNDO game just wasn't worth the fuss. It was a failure, like everything else he had ever tried to do. How could he have thought that anybody, least of all Sam Snyder, would want to steal it? Bitterly disillusioned and in a thoroughly bad temper, Tim finally turned his back on Doggo and the green bottle, and marched off home.

When he got there, he found Mrs Figgins explaining to his mother over the front fence that a neighbour had just been rushed to hospital after eating what she had thought were mushrooms.

'A terrible case of 'uman error,' Mrs Figgins was explaining with grim satisfaction. Then she spotted Tim, and cried in thunderstruck surprise: 'Well, bless us, here's your Tim! Why's he moping about with nothing to do, on a nice day like this?'

'Why are you moping about with nothing to do?' Tim's mother asked Tim. 'You could be finding that formica, for a start.'

Whereupon Tim's face changed from dull angry red to bright angry red, and he turned and marched back the way he had just come, calling rudely over his shoulder: 'As a matter of fact, I've got plenty to do. Me and Doggo's just started a Reign of Terror.'

'Cheek!' Mrs Evans called after him. 'You wait till your dad comes home!'

6
Even More Instant Death

Sam Snyder was sorting Bingo cards into bundles of twenty, but at the sound of the doorbell he looked up. Tim and Doggo edged cautiously into the shop, Doggo deftly turning the OPEN sign to CLOSED behind his back.

Sam Snyder frowned with instant suspicion, but before he had time to utter a word Doggo whipped out the bottle from underneath his anorak and placed it strategically on the counter.

'Oh, not you again!' Sam Snyder groaned at Tim.

'You remember him and his REDUNDO board, then?' began Doggo pleasantly, swivelling the INSTANT DEATH label round to a spot where Sam's gaze was bound to fall upon it.

'Remember his board? I've never had the chance to forget it!' spluttered Sam. 'But I can promise you this, if I hear any more about it there'll be trouble. I've already told you I don't know what's happened to it. So you can go away and stop pestering me. And take that sticky bottle of bubble-blower with you.'

'Bubble-blower?' shrieked Doggo in indignant disbelief. 'That's not bubble-blower. . . . '

But he got no further, for suddenly a curtain at the rear of the shop was swished aside and a plump, warm, beaming Mrs Snyder bounced into view.

'Couldn't help overhearing,' she admitted. 'And maybe I can help if you're looking for a board. I found one lying about when I was vacuuming the shop. It didn't look like genuine stock; it had no name or address on, and it was in the way. So I threw it out.'

'Threw it out?' echoed Tim, aghast.

'Well, I propped it up against the dustbin; it was too big to fit inside. You could have had it back, son, only they've been for the rubbish this morning. I'm ever so sorry!'

Tim's shoulders sagged. 'Oh well, that's that, then!' He was now prepared to forget the whole thing, having at least been reassured that his idea was not stolen. Some day, perhaps, he could start again.

'No need for you to apologise,' Sam told his wife sternly. 'It was the lad's own fault for leaving that board where he did. Kids are far too pushy and cheeky these days. Think they can do just what they like.' He seized the GLOLOX bottle and waved it in the air. 'There's an example! Look at that, plonked down without a thought! It's left a great, sticky patch on my counter, has that!' Still clutching the bottle, Sam dived under the counter for a cloth to wipe up the mess.

Meantime, Mrs Snyder had her eye on Tim. 'Oh, bless him! He's upset!' she crooned sympathetically. 'I never thought that board would mean so much to anybody or I wouldn't have thrown it out. Invented it yourself, did you, son? Well, if it's any comfort, you did all right, except that people don't want to make fun of tragedies like unemployment. You'll have to think of a fresh idea. But keep trying, because I reckon you've a flair!'

Tim looked up in amazement. Mrs Snyder had actually liked his game! He could not remember anybody ever praising him before and could not stop himself blushing with pleasure. She was wrong about REDUNDO being too tragic, though. What could be more tragic than hounding a king to death, as in chess; or being told to GO TO JAIL; or falling prey to some nasty, deadly snake, just when you're at the top of your ladder?

'Tell you what, why don't you two come through and have a glass of orange juice and a slice of cake? It's the least I can do to make up for what I can only describe as a genuine human error.'

Mrs Snyder held the curtain aside invitingly, affording a glimpse of a comfortable sitting-room with plenty of fat, shiny cushions, plastic roses in a vase and a radio softly playing. As the boys seemed hesitant, she encouraged them: 'Don't mind my husband! His bark's worse than his bite. I expect he's mad at himself for not keeping a better eye on your game.'

Sam, rising up from the depths of the counter like the Loch Ness Monster, protested loudly at this, belligerently brandishing the GLOLOX. That was the moment at which his wife first caught sight of the bottle. She froze in mid-sentence and turned pale, eyes widening in a horrified face. Then, with an awful moan, she half-collapsed against the wall, pointing with trembling finger at the dark green bottle.

'P-put it d-down carefully, S-Sam,' she managed to stammer. 'D-don't bang it or j-jerk it about.'

'Oh, it's all right,' Tim reassured his new friend. 'It's only shampoo.'

Doggo glared murderously at Tim, but Mrs Snyder was not listening. She was staring at her husband in pure terror and whispering: 'The news-flash! Didn't you hear the news-flash?'

'How could I hear a news-flash when I've been in the shop all morning?' Sam snapped irritably. 'What news-flash? What are you talking about?'

Mrs Snyder took a shaky breath. 'You know they've got couriers at Helmuth, running messages for the scientists? Well, one of them couriers disappeared this morning when he was out delivering a bottle full of highly dangerous dark green liquid. It didn't say what the stuff actually was, but they were making such a fuss,

it must be something terrible. They said nobody was to touch that bottle if they found it, not for love nor money!' She turned distractedly to the boys. 'Where did you pick it up?'

'I don't believe this!' Doggo groaned, glimpsing what could have becn wonderful possibilities.

But Tim retorted, '*I* do! It's just my rotten sort of luck!'

7

Tragedy Strikes Home

There was only one thing to do, and Doggo did it. He grabbed the bottle (which Sam Snyder had set down in bewilderment on the counter) and fled, dragging Tim with him before the lad had time to protest. They were halfway to Doggo's house by the time Mr Snyder had finished dialling 999.

'What do we do now?' Tim wondered miserably. 'We aren't half going to be in trouble. It was stupid to run off with the bottle like that. It just makes us look

guilty.' His chief regret was that nice Mrs Snyder, who had taken an interest in him, must now regard him as a loathsome, despicable terrorist.

'We haven't done anything wrong that I know of,' maintained Doggo stubbornly. 'We never even made any threats. We didn't have a chance. All we did was plonk a bottle of shampoo down on Sam Snyder's counter. If he thought it was something else, that's his look-out. And how were we to know some daft courier was going to lose his bottle at the same time? Proper careless, he must have been.'

'Yeah, I hope he gets his share of what's coming,' Tim said bitterly. 'He deserves the sack and at least ten years in the Tower of London.'

'Good thing I kept that strip of label when I cut it off,' said Doggo. 'Did a very neat job on that with one of my dad's special shop razor-blades. All we have to do now is to stick the strip on again, put the shampoo back in our bathroom cabinet and lie low.'

'Lie low where?'

Doggo thought for a minute, then he said: 'There's one place that's pretty deserted in the holidays, and that's school. We could hide in there for a bit, just till they've found their precious bottle. The fuss will soon die down then, and they might even forget about us altogether.'

'School will be locked up,' said Tim, who was by no

means eager to go back there before he had to. But Doggo thought they could manage to get in somehow.

'Leave it to me!' he said.

However, by now Tim was thoroughly fed up. Enough had been left to Doggo as it was, and look where his efforts had got them!

'Why don't we just go and confess, and get it over with?' Tim suggested gloomily.

'Who to? The police? You must be joking!' Doggo could scarcely believe his ears. 'I'm not confessing to anything, especially when I haven't done it.'

'Well, all right, let's do something positive instead of just crawling into a hole and hiding. Something that will put us in the right again with everyone. Let's find that missing courier—and the bottle. They must be around here somewhere.'

'Hey!' cried Doggo, brightening. 'That's not a bad idea! Might be quite an adventure, in fact.' He looked at his watch. 'There's a news bulletin in ten minutes. Maybe that will tell us more about it, so that we'll know where to start looking.' He ran into the house and turned on the radio.

The two of them fretted impatiently through a whole dreary weather forecast, and an even drearier political wrangle, before the item was even mentioned, but at last there it was.

'Late this morning it was reported that a courier

from the highly secret Helmuth Research Establishment had failed to keep an assignment at the companion laboratory on the moors between Whitsend and Doomsbury. It is believed that his car, which was delivering a bottle of highly dangerous liquid, was hijacked, the courier taken hostage and the bottle stolen. The car was later found abandoned in a remote spot on the moors.' There then followed a description of the bottle and a warning not to handle it if it was found. 'Anyone with any information about the earlier movements of this white Mini Metro registration number. . . .'

Doggo, ready with pen and paper, began eagerly scribbling down the registration number, but before he had finished Tim was careering round the room like a lunatic.

'That's my dad's car!' he was shouting. 'My dad must be that courier! He's been kidnapped!'

'Oh, no! It's one bloomin' shock after another!' moaned Doggo. 'What was it you wished on that courier? The sack and at least ten years in the Tower of London?'

'Stop clowning—my dad could be dead!' yelled Tim, who was desperately trying to take in all this staggering information. He had not even known his dad was a courier, and now there Mr Evans was, in the power of some madman with a genuine bottle of

Instant Death, while Tim's mother stood poised on the verge of widowhood. The most sickening thing about it was that Tim could not help feeling it was all his fault.

8

Reign of Terror

Tim ran home at once, followed at a respectful distance by Doggo, who did not want to intrude upon the family's grief but felt he would like to be near, just in case he could help. So Doggo hung around the Evans' garden gate chewing his nails and kicking bits of gravel, while Tim rushed into the house.

Aunt Maisie and Uncle Cyril were in the kitchen, commiserating with Tim's mother.

'Came round right away to see what we could do,' said Uncle Cyril, all solemn for once.

'Well, you can keep Mrs Figgins out for a start,' Tim's mother wailed hysterically as she spotted an eager face hovering outside the kitchen window.

'Would you like me to drive up on to the moors and look for Lewis?'

'That's a super idea, Uncle Cyril! Me and Doggo will come with you.'

Since Mrs Evans was too upset by now to offer an opinion—and in fact was being led off to bed by Aunt Maisie—away went Cyril and Tim, collecting Doggo at the gate.

'I don't know about taking you kids,' Uncle Cyril worried. 'We might run into trouble.'

'Three pairs of eyes are better than one,' said Tim. 'And your own eyes will be watching the road, anyway. Doggo and me can look out of both sides of the car, and if Dad's up there we'll spot him.'

'I've got really good eyesight,' Doggo claimed. 'My mum once said she reckoned I'd got double vision.'

'That was when you said you'd given her twenty pence change instead of tenpence,' Tim reminded him, but he said it quietly so that Uncle Cyril could not hear.

'All right—get in, then!' Uncle Cyril had just opened the rear door of his car when a police vehicle drew up on the opposite side of the road.

Another half-minute, and they could have been away!

'Excuse me, sir,' a police officer addressed himself politely to Uncle Cyril, 'but we're looking for two boys named Timothy Evans and'—here he consulted his notebook incredulously—'Eustace Barker. As you have just emerged from Timothy Evans's house accompanied by two young gentlement in the correct age-range, I assume . . . .'

'You assume right, officer,' sighed Uncle Cyril. Turning to the boys, he asked what the dickens they had been up to now.

The police officer explained. 'I'm afraid I shall have

to ask them to accompany me to the station. Just routine, you understand, sir; probably all a waste of time, but in a case of national security we have to make absolutely sure.'

'Honest, officer, it was only shampoo!' insisted Doggo for the umpteenth time. 'I can run home and fetch the bottle if you like.'

'We *have* got lots of shampoo at our house,' agreed Doggo's mother, who had had to be fetched before the police questioning could begin. 'Though I must say I never noticed any missing.'

'That's because I put it back,' said Doggo.

'What did you want shampoo for, anyway?' his mother could not help asking. In normal circumstances she practically had to tie Doggo to the sink before he would consent to having his hair washed.

'We were going to blow bubbles with it.'

The police officer grinned, which made Doggo feel even more shame-faced. Blowing bubbles was kids' stuff. But what else could Doggo have said? He only hoped that Tim, being interrogated in another room, would be inspired to give the same answer.

Alas! Tim had crumpled under the weight of grief and guilt. He had lost his dad, his game and his only adult ally, Mrs Snyder; and he wished he had never heard of GLOLOX. To crown it all, on the way here in the police car, when he was helpless to do anything about it, he had spotted four dustmen rattling a dice-shaker excitedly round his REDUNDO board as they took their tea-break on a grass verge. In a scarcely audible voice, Tim admitted miserably:

'That bottle was a sort of blackmail.'

'Blackmail, eh?'

The police officer, who had just read a rambling

report from the policewoman sent to see Tim's prostrate mother, now frowned thoughtfully at the long, red weal on Tim's neck.

'I suppose this is all part of the Reign of Terror your mother's been going on about?'

9

Eureka!

In the police station there was a sudden flurry of activity. An important telephone message had just come in. Lewis Evans, the missing Helmuth courier, had turned up at his destination after all, several hours late but still in possession of the all important bottle. What is more, he was claiming not to have been hi-jacked at all. Such a tale, he insisted, was too fantastic for words. Yet the tale he eventually told to reporters who swarmed into the laboratory was even more fan-tastic.

Lewis Evans possessed, he explained modestly, a fine tenor voice and had often sung in such great works as Handel's *Messiah.* But lately, what with shift-work and family commitments and jobs around the house (like fitting a formica top on his wife's washer, for instance) he didn't have time to belong to a choir. So whenever his day's assignment took him up on to the moors—as it often did, Helmuth's companion laboratory being situated between Whitsend and Doomsbury—he would get out of the car for ten minutes or so at the remotest spot he could find, fill his lungs with good, clean air and then let rip with a couple of arias, or the 'Soldiers' Chorus' from *Faust*, a practice which disturbed nobody but the sheep.

That was exactly what he had done today. The only difference was that today he had accidentally locked his keys in the car when he got out to sing, and had therefore had to walk the last, long, difficult moorland stretch to the laboratory, sinking up to his knees in a peat-bog on the way. Luckily, the Helmuth product,

the vital bottle, had been nestling safely in his jacket pocket all the time, and had been duly delivered.

'Wasn't that a dangerous thing to do?' an outraged reporter cried. 'Gallivanting about on craggy, boggy moors with a lethal bottle in your pocket?'

'Downright irresponsible, I call it!' another reporter shouted, to a chorus of 'hear, hear's.

Whereupon Lewis, looking genuinely puzzled, cried, 'Lethal? What's so lethal about a cure for the common cold? Even if it does turn out to be another dud?'

Well!

There had been, it seemed a mix-up. Some overworked publicity officer at Helmuth had given out the wrong information in a panic when Lewis Evans was first reported missing. It turned out to be another member of staff, a Leonard Evans, now happily on his way to Porton Down, who was actually in charge of the dark green lethal stuff.

Of course he was! The really dangerous stuff, as Lewis Evans later assured the world in a television interview, was not shuttled around the country in Mini Metros, but packed inside well-lined, well-protected crates in special spill-proof vans.

'They wouldn't trust me with it, in any case,' he was forced to admit. 'I'm only a Courier Grade Four, not Grade One like Leonard Evans.'

Tim, who was sampling the novelty of watching his own dad on television, felt a sudden leap of the spirits at this. That would put paid to his mother's smug hints to the neighbours! 'Courier Grade Four' was a far cry from the Chief Research Scientist she was always trying to suggest. In fact, 'Courier Grade Four' was barely adequate for making one's mark on the world at all, television interviews notwithstanding. Surely Tim could do better than that? A tiny bubble of euphoria rose somewhere in the depths of Tim and began to work its way upwards towards his brain.

'So, are we to understand, then,' the television interviewer was now demanding of Lewis Evans, 'that this whole unfortunate episode, this full-scale panic, this numbing shock to an already nervous nation, was nothing more than a couple of stupid mistakes?'

Tim's dad grinned sheepishly at the camera.

'Afraid so!' he admitted. 'You'll just have to look on it as a double dose of simple human error. After all, that's life in a nutshell, isn't it?'

This was the moment at which the bubble reached Tim's brain and burst like the Dawn of Enlightenment. Radiant, he leapt from his seat, projecting his arms, his whole body, his very soul in a joyous 'Hallelujah Chorus' towards the ceiling.

For Tim Evans had just thought of a wonderful new game called UMANERRA. Two or more players

shook dice and moved around a board, attempting to reach OLD AGE without lighting upon any one of a number of 'human error' obstacles, ranging in stupidity and horror from . . . .

Tim reached eagerly for pen and paper.

Well it was fun…

ISBN: 1-4392-0336-9
ISBN-13: 9781439203361